ROOTS2Wellness

Unearth the Root Cause of Dis-ease
and Discover Your Route to Wellness

Janet E Verney

ISBN: 1501000551
ISBN 13: 9781501000553
Library of Congress Control Number: 2014915846
CreateSpace Independent Publishing Platform
North Charleston, South Carolina

Cover art & design by Heather Rhodes
Interior artwork by Heather Rhodes
Author photo by Heather Rhodes

Endorsements:

"Janet Verney's story is an inspiration to others to 'walk the walk' that she has walked and talked about so well. This book is a valuable resource for those who live with chronic illnesses who are seeking a path to health."

Kathleen C. Laundy, PsyD, LMFT, Family Psychologist and
Author of *Building School-Based Collaborative Mental Health Teams:*
A Systems Approach to Student Achievement

"Janet Verney suffered with a debilitating undiagnosed disease that led her down a path of frustration and sadness. It wasn't until she dug deep into her life to discover the root cause, that she could begin the process of healing. If you are lost and needing support, follow Janet's guidance and let her lead the way toward helping you on your own journey to health and wellness."

Andrea Beaman, HHC/Chef

"Regardless of the number of our years, taking care of our health and well-being is essential. While I know this and want to do it, I have often thought the path to achieve healing and health a complicated subject. In her important book, Janet maps out an insightful road map to mind/body well-being. With her guidance, I feel prepared to take on more responsibility for achieving mine."

Carmen Lund, Artist and Creativity Coach

"I love the tree metaphor in which Janet shares unearthing her past in order to find peace, love and acceptance. She plants the idea that one can change their biology by changing one's thoughts. She heals herself by sending forgiveness, love and gratitude to the root of her illness. This is a remarkable account of perseverance and discovery, which leads to the reclamation of health."

Dr. Jackie Campisi, Hippocrates Health Institute Graduate;
Healing stage 4 metastatic cancer holistically.

Special Notes to You

Thank you for purchasing this book. May my words, ideas, and experiences help you in some way, large or small! I know your day is filled with a blizzard of activity, so I kept this book short and precise with your hectic calendar in mind. If you crave more, go to www.roots2wellness.com and check out my blog, recipe cards, and other tips and treats.

While reading this book, you may want to keep a blank journal handy to make notes and to do the various activities throughout the book. I encourage you to find a journal with a cover that speaks to you, or pick up one with a plain cover and make it your own by creating a collage of pictures and words that represent those things in life that are important to you.

The information presented in this book is meant to encourage you to improve your health, and to support you in your healing journey. It is not a substitute for medical advice, nor is it an attempt to diagnose or treat any health conditions. Please work in partnership with your health care practitioners to navigate your healing journey.

In wellness,
Janet

A Mother's Inspiration

A beat-up laminate table, and drawers filled with treasures,
set the stage to ignite the magic of a child's imagination.

Gloria Hess Fawber
March 17, 1929–August 16, 2012

I dedicate this book in loving memory of my mom,
who kindled in me a lifelong, artistic, creative passion.

Contents

My Dis-Ease, My Gift

© heather rhodes

Chapter 1

"Within every challenge lies an opportunity for growth."

Sound asleep, cozy in the comfort of my bed, I suddenly realize I can't breathe. Unfortunately, this is an all-too-familiar scene in my life, one that scares the hell out of me every time it happens. It's like an alarm going off, making me bolt to attention. In a flash I go from sleeping to sitting up, desperate to get my breathing going. I'm then afraid to go back to sleep, afraid I may not wake up. This was the pattern of my life for more than twenty dark and confusing years.

Dialing back to my early twenties, I'm living in an apartment in Hartford, CT. One beautiful, sunny morning I decide to go for a run. As I start, my chest is heavy and, with each step I take, it gets harder and harder to breathe. I try to ignore it and hope the feeling will go away, but it keeps getting worse. I begin obsessing about what's wrong and why this is happening to me; at the same time, I feel a bit of panic bubbling up in my chest from not being able to take a full, deep breath. Later in the day I head to the doctor, who diagnoses me with a bad case of bronchitis. At least that's what he thinks it is.

The doctor prescribes an antibiotic, which seems to help a little, yet the congestion is still there. In fact, it never goes away. This health crisis is suddenly front and center in my life. I go to doctor after doctor, and each one has a diagnosis that is subsequently disproven by another. I feel discouraged and, with each infection, more and more afraid of what is to come.

My primary care physician (PCP) insists the problem is asthma, and proceeds to prescribe a multitude of meds. I take them faithfully, even though it doesn't feel right. (You know that feeling down deep in your gut when something just isn't right.) In the long run, the medicines make me feel worse. The prednisone has me all hyped up, the albuterol makes me feel jittery, and the theophylline is making me feel lightheaded and shaky on my feet. That's when I begin seeing a pulmonologist. After several breathing tests, he rules out asthma, I take myself off the meds, and shortly thereafter I find a new PCP.

The infections are getting worse and more frequent, and are greatly interfering with my day-to-day work and play. I never know when I am going to have a bad day, so it is hard to plan ahead. I end up canceling events (a date with a friend, an outing to some place fun) or calling in sick to work. I love public speaking, yet I am embarrassed by my cough. I am often asked if it is a smoker's cough, and then I go into my spiel about having an undiagnosed cough. When I explain that we don't know what it is, I sense judgment in the questioner's eyes and self-doubt creeps in; I feel like one of the "misfit toys." By now, I have been told by a few docs that maybe it's all in my head. More self-doubt, some sadness, and a big dose of self-pity add up to a feeling of depression.

In my late twenties, I am still suffering from one infection after another, and the antibiotics are becoming more and more problematic. One gives me a head-to-toe rash that takes days to go away, another causes me to vomit, and yet another puts hives the size of quarters all over my body. The hives last fifteen torturous days! The PCP on call during this episode tells me I need to "chill out," and prescribes Valium. Feeling insulted and demoralized by this treatment plan, I seek out a dermatologist, who prescribes antihistamines, terry cloth towel soaks to cool the hives, and a rubdown with a topical med called Sarna to numb the pain and the itch. Although I find some relief from the hives, my lungs continue to rattle and wheeze.

Feeling like I am drowning in a living nightmare, I waffle between determination (to figure this thing out and fix it) and surrender (feeling like just giving up). On some of my darker days, thoughts of suicide creep in, yet I manage to rise above the temptation and keep forging forward. Pulling myself up by the proverbial bootstraps, I see a pulmonologist recommended to me by a friend who is a family doc. He does many tests, including scans.

I sit on the cold, hard examination table, waiting anxiously for the pulmonologist to return, all the while imaging the worst possible diagnoses. He enters the room and, with a concerned look on his face, delivers the news that I have bronchiectasis, which is, essentially, damage to the lower bronchiolar tubes of the lungs, with no real known cause. He goes on to tell me that this condition will get worse with time, creeping further up the airways, and that there is no cure; the standard treatment is more antibiotics. A wave of emotion hits me; I feel shock and disbelief, and an overwhelming sense of fear once again consumes me.

With my condition getting worse, my pulmonologist refers me to another pulmonologist, who is reputed to be one of the best in the state. This new doc tells me that the only way to really know what's going on with my lungs is to go in and take a look. So, after getting more details about the procedure, I agree to have my first bronchoscopy. And the nightmare continues.... I enter the sterile surgical room feeling cold in my skimpy hospital gown. I am asked to sit on the table while they start an IV to give me some meds to keep me relaxed. They convince me it's best to be awake during this procedure so I can assist in the process.

I don't care what anyone says, there aren't enough drugs coursing through my veins to keep me relaxed and calm. First I gargle with a disgusting liquid that tastes nasty and instantly makes my tongue go numb. Then I experience terror as the anesthesiologist comes at me with extra-long forceps, holding a wad of gauze soaked in some more numbing solution. He proceeds to inch this wad of stuff down my throat to continue the numbing process, but when he brings the forceps back up, the gauze does not come with it. I am now numb, but choking on the wad of gauze lodged in my throat, with no ability to get it out on my own since everything is frozen from the drugs. A sudden chaos ensues as an army of folks dressed in green surrounds me, trying to extract their blunder from my throat. One of them is talking to me softly, telling me to stay calm and that I am going to be all right. After what seems like an eternity, the gauze is removed and the procedure begins.

A long, snake-like instrument is carefully maneuvered down my throat and into my lungs. I can feel a slight sensation of it being there, while staring up at the doc who is intensely looking with one eye down this high-tech scope into the depths of my lungs. My panic subsides, yet it's lurking at the edge of my medically-suppressed emotions as I lay back onto the surgical table. I fall asleep at some point, and then I awake to one of the most painful sore throats I have ever encountered. The conclusion—it is not bronchiectasis; there is no damage to my lungs, yet there is no conclusive diagnosis.

The pulmonologist recommends removing part of my lung to dissect and study it.

Say what? Uh, I don't think so! First you tell me there is no damage to my lungs, then you tell me you want to cut out a chunk! No way, no how! This outrageous suggestion makes me realize that the word of a doctor is not the word of God, and not always the best course of action. It wakes me up to playing a leading role in my own health, life, and happiness. Believe it or not, I stay on with this doc a short while, and learn all that I can from him. He has another theory—that I may have an unusual case of cystic fibrosis (CF), and he proceeds to refer me to a pediatric pulmonologist who specializes in CF. So off I go to see my third pulmonologist.

The pediatric pulmonologist is not only incredibly knowledgeable in her specialty; she is equally compassionate and supportive of her patients. It is the first time I feel heard, understood, and fully supported by a doctor. As a result I trust her completely, while maintaining my newfound sense of being fully in charge of my determined healing journey. So when she recommends another bronchoscopy, I only slightly freak. She promises that I will be out for the entire procedure, and will not feel a thing. I land in the pediatric recovery room—a night-and-day difference from the last bronch experience! I awake with the familiar sore throat, but I am surrounded by teddy bears and hanging mobiles.

In addition, the pediatric pulmonologist runs some blood work and does a sweat test, a common salt test associated with diagnosing CF. During the bronch, she extracted a bunch of fluid from my lungs, which was chalk white. Further testing shows the fluid has a 25 percent level of fat cells, which are not supposed to be there. With this new information, she refers me to another pulmonologist at Yale, who is both a research doc and a clinician. Together, we find a lab in California that sequences my entire CF gene, which comes back completely normal. It is a double-edged result; I'm happy I do not have CF, yet frustrated I still don't have a diagnosis.

Having completed her CF evaluation on me, the pediatric pulmonologist passes me on to my fourth pulmonologist. My new pulmonologist leaves no stone unturned, and proceeds to test for extremely unusual and rare diseases. He works with other specialists to cover all avenues. I see an endocrinologist, an allergist, a cardiologist, an ophthalmologist, a doc who specializes in environmental-related diseases, and more! These specialists each test my blood, take a history of my health asking a gazillion questions, and then perform additional tests, some more obnoxious than others. The worst is from the ophthalmologist, who looks for Behçet's disease by attempting to put what looks like a socket wrench around my eyeball to view the blood vessels behind my eye. I say attempts, because my eye muscle will not cooperate and keeps closing on the wrench-like object, not allowing it to do its job! With each test I am hopeful yet terrified.

I feel alone. It's easy to withdraw, yet I tell my story to anyone who will listen, in hopes that someone will know something that will lead to a diagnosis, a treatment, and ultimately, a cure. I discover in this process that everyone has a story, and although it may not involve an undiagnosed disease, the resulting pain, fear, and trauma is just as real. I find strength in knowing I'm really not alone.

Many years go by with more tests, more infections, more scary nights, more missed life, and the fear continues to build. I now know when an infection is setting in, as I get a "fibromyalgia" feeling throughout my body, a fatigue so thick it knocks me off my feet. That's when the gunk I cough up starts turning an awful shade of army green, and it has a smell and taste that is indescribably disgusting. This is when I know I have no choice but to start another round of antibiotic treatment.

Allergic reactions to antibiotics now create fungal infections throughout my body, and send me to the ER. After long nights of coughing, I aggravate the cartilage in my chest; it hurts to take a breath, and I feel as if there is a brick sitting on me. The years of antibiotics affect my gut, and result in what's known as irritable bowel syndrome, causing an array of uncomfortable and embarrassing symptoms.

On one visit to the pulmonologist, he tells me I have developed in my lungs a colonization of staph, which at any time can take my life! He proceeds to give me his cell phone number, his pager, and his e-mail address, and tells me to contact him immediately should I feel any unusual symptoms. My level of fear has now escalated, and I wonder daily if this will be my last day. I begin to obsess over every little symptom, and I question whether this is the end. The fear is all consuming.

My daily routine begins and ends with twenty minutes hooked up to a $16,000 respiratory compression vest, and nebulizing a 7 percent saline solution. This is what it takes to clear the gunk from my lungs. In addition, one week a month I take an inhaled antibiotic called TOBI, at $6,000 for a month's supply! I become very dependent on this regimen just to be able to breathe. Even with all of this treatment, sometimes I still sound like a percolator, which prevents me from taking part in group activities like yoga and meditation, for fear of sounding like some diseased gremlin. It also curbs my gypsy desire for travel, as the vest alone weighs over forty pounds, and the TOBI requires refrigeration. (The fact that it's a liquid makes the process of airport security a nightmare.) I am trapped in a routine that feels like a prison to me. I dream of what life would be like without all this hullabaloo.

I discover a program at the National Institutes of Health (NIH) called the Undiagnosed Diseases Program (UDP). After I research it, I ask my doc to make a referral to the program. I am accepted, as one of a hundred patients in the country that year, to attend this program.

I get on a train to Maryland with my sister and head to the NIH. We arrive and go through a thorough search; it is high security and very intimidating. We head to our accommodations, which are extremely nice, allowing me to be an out-patient on the campus. That is, until a member of the admissions team reads my records, and sees that I have a colonization of staph in my lungs. They proceed to quarantine me in a sterile hospital room, alone, not allowed to leave without permission. Anyone coming to my room to visit is required to wear protective gear, which further makes me feel like a diseased gremlin.

Every morning I awake at 5:00 a.m. to have eight tubes of blood taken. The day proceeds with one test after another, interviews with various doctors, and lots of waiting to see and hear results. Each day the residents and interns make their rounds, stopping at my door to ask many questions. In total, I have a team of about fifty docs studying my case, looking at every result, and asking ever more questions as they dive deeper into my case. This program is very much like the TV show *House*, although at the end of the week, I don't walk away with a diagnosis.

The day before I am to leave the NIH, I have a transbronchial biopsy. Before the procedure I am told that, unlike the other bronchs I've had, this one holds a higher risk for puncturing my lung, and if that happens, they will need to punch a hole through my chest to reinflate my lung. I am beyond scared, and proceed to call my doc back home and ask for his opinion. He encourages me to allow the test to move forward. He tells me I'm in good hands and have come this far, and while at the NIH I should take advantage of every test I can. In addition to undergoing the transbronch, I get just about every part of my body scanned and examined. I begin to empathize with lab rats and other critters used in the process of all good science. I don't know how I would have gotten through this without my sister being there, supporting me, making me laugh, and giving me words of encouragement.

Although my lungs do not deflate, my sense of hope does as I leave Maryland after a week of torture without any new information that leads to a diagnosis. Now on the train home, exhausted and depleted, I am coughing up blood from the procedure the day before. I become silent. Although the space around me is filled with the sounds of others chatting, the chugging along of the train engines, and the clicking and clanking of activity, it all disappears. I go within, someplace deep, wondering what the future holds.

I begin to question everything. Will I even make it home to see my family? I certainly don't feel as if I will. What's next? Can I really go through more testing? How can I live like this when it keeps getting worse? What can I change to make it better?—this is the ultimate question! This is the question that serves as the turning point for me to live in a state of wellness, rather than dis-ease. I am more determined than ever to shift my focus from finding a diagnosis, to unearthing the root cause of my illness, taking control of what I can control, and leaving the rest up to a higher power.

My journey to wellness has been an evolution through many years. The journey continues today. I'll describe the steps throughout this book. The first step was to take control, to stop being a *recipient* of health care, and become a *partner* in my own health care. From this point on, I would only work with doctors who agreed to partner with me, by listening to my concerns, respecting my opinions, and honoring my boundaries.

While I continued with traditional health care, I decided to engage nontraditional health care providers. From them I learned to dig deep and "unearth" the nonbiological roots of my dis-ease. You'll read more about this in chapter 2.

Along the way, I also learned that only I can remove many of the obstacles that impede my health—things that fall into categories like toxic relationships, addictions, and forgiveness. Others are there to support me, but it is ultimately up to me to weed out such obstacles. More about this in chapter 3.

Chapter 4 it is all about nourishing your roots to strengthen your core so you can bloom. It is broken into six sections, detailing what I have learned and how you may apply it to your own healing.

A major turning point for me was in discovering that it is my responsibility to choose self-talk that builds me up and supports my goals, rather than fearful and negative thinking. I learned that I can literally change my biology by changing my thoughts. In chapter 4, section 1, you'll read about the science and thought leaders who opened my eyes to this truth.

I spent time at a healing institute, where I gained tremendous knowledge about the way food and lifestyle choices play key roles in our health (or lack thereof). I learned we can change our biology by the food choices we make. Through the exploration of food and nutrition, key ingredients became a primary path for my healing. My passion for food and nutrition grows every day, as I see the difference food can make in the healing process. In chapter 4, section 2, I'll give you the highlights I learned about food and nutrition, including a couple of sample recipes.

As I learned about how toxic foods affect us and cause an imbalance in our bodies, I also discovered the hidden health risks of many of the products we put on our skin, and the chemicals we use to clean our homes. I learned to clean up not only my diet, but the environment around me. Chapter 4, section 3, provides an overview about self-care and the environment.

Chapter 4, section 4, is about movement. In my adult life, which is very active and busy, exercise has never been a high priority, so this chapter describes tips I use to keep moving to stay healthy, elevating movement to the top of the list

As I've journeyed toward wellness, my most profound realization has been that spirituality, love, and creativity are one. For most of my life, I had felt devoid of any spiritual connection. This changed when my health eroded, and I sought out a higher power, which I call God. Chapter 4, section 5 is about love, energy, and spirit.

I believe that each of us has the inner power to heal. That doesn't mean we need to (or should even try to) go it alone. Chapter 4, section 6, is about how to navigate outside resources and support to optimize your health.

Chapter 5 ties it all together. I wrote my whole book, as well as this final chapter, trying to share my own journey and the lessons I've learned along the way, so that your journey might be easier. Over time, I've come to realize that my dis-ease has, in many ways, been a gift, providing me with many learning opportunities and the chance to meet many gifted and wonderful people. It led me to become a certified Health Coach, providing the tools to help others, like you, improve your overall health and happiness. So many of the tools I have gained as a result of my illness have become part of my daily practice. These practices have given me the ability to be off all my lung machines and medications. Now and then I still have a flare-up, yet day by day I am so much better. Now, rather than living with a focus on managing symptoms of my illness, I am just an ordinary girl making magic, living healthy ever after!

May my experiences, ideas, and activities inspire you to embrace your own route to wellness, and may you live healthy ever after!

Unearth & Address Your Root Cause

Chapter 2

*"Beneath the earth a tiny seed transforms, reaching
for the light and radiating a beautiful bloom."*

believe that at some point in their life, everyone will receive a wake-up call—for some, the call will be more devastating than for others. Some will listen to that call and improve their lives for the better, and others clearly will miss the call. A wake-up call can come in a variety of shapes and sizes. It can be an illness or a divorce, the loss of a job or the loss of a loved one. Whatever its form, the wake-up call serves as that pivotal event in our lives that reaches deep into the gut, into the essence of who we are, and asks us to rise above it, make changes, and wake up to life!

In my case, an illness led me to my wake-up call, my call to action. So the journey began, and I explored many avenues of healing. My healing journey began with food, and although food plays a critical role in our health, it is not the end-all to living well. You can eat all the broccoli you want, but if you don't uncover the root cause of the imbalance in your body, the broccoli will simply give you gas! I realized this by trial and error, and continued to seek new ways to heal. Each one provided certain health benefits, yet I continued to get sick.

We need to dig deeper sometimes to unearth that root cause—this is where true healing begins. I knew I was severely abused as a child, and yet I could not recall many of the actual memories. It was not until I turned thirty that little snapshots of the abuse started popping into my head. I would be going through my morning routine, when all of a sudden flashes of memories would come out of the blue, and a rush of adrenaline would surge through me. I felt a sense of panic and, eventually, full-fledged panic attacks would ensue. There were days I felt possessed by someone or something other than myself.

I learned from a friend and practitioner that when we experience extreme trauma to the mind or body, this gets stored in our cells and will erupt from time to time. This was happening to me. Whenever I removed my belt while getting undressed, I would feel this surge of adrenaline shoot through me, not really understanding where it was coming from. The belt was my dad's tool for disciplining his children, and I learned later in life that I experienced this punishment nightly due to my rambunctious behavior. Now when I feel this adrenaline surging, I know where it is coming from; I am able to reassure myself that I am safe, and that I will not allow anyone to harm me. The sensation quickly dissipates and I move on.

The thought had not occurred to me that my past experience with abuse, and a rather turbulent childhood, could play key roles in the development of my dis-ease; that feeling invisible, alone, invalidated, and unworthy could actually contribute to my illness and be destructive to my health. Negative thoughts and feelings erode our health, and unless they are addressed head-on, the broccoli will simply be a Band-Aid, not a cure for true healing.

The panic attacks were interfering with my day-to-day life, and gave me no choice but to address them. I connected with a friend and mentor, who quickly became my lifeline to releasing old hurts and recognizing that I was so much more than I thought I was. This was the beginning of a new sense of self, one that stems from self-love, self-care, and understanding.

As I describe my turbulent past, I imagine I can hear you say, "I can relate to that," or "I felt that way when...," or "Wow, I recall when _____ happened, I felt like _____." Was there something that happened long ago that has left you feeling "less than," or wounded in some way? Did you experience a traumatic injury that has reshaped who you are, and how you feel about yourself? I encourage you to get out the microscope or the magnifying glass and look closely at some of your life's events, which may be influencing how you respond to life and how you feel about who you are as a person. Although the answers lie within you, working with a professional counselor or coach will help you unravel this thread and greatly support your healing journey. I offer a word of caution, though. There is a difference between utilizing the services of a professional to support your healing journey and believing that any one practitioner or pill will solve the problem. As I said before, the answers lie within, but getting a little support to unearth the root cause helps to create a route to wellness, and provides a solid foundation from which to grow. It is priceless when you remain at the helm of your own healing.

Okay, this is your turning point! You are making a choice to unearth this root cause that is preventing you from healing and living in wellness. As I went through this process, there were many tears. It's not easy dredging up the past, or facing a current issue head-on. I often felt ashamed, wondering how I could have allowed this, or what I did to deserve this abuse and turbulence. That is why working with a dedicated professional is so helpful. When someone else can see through the mess to the true essence of you, which is pure love, they can help you see the light through the thick trees of the forest. Know that there are many routes to take in supporting this journey; do what feels right to you, and keep trying various forms of healing until you find what works best for you.

There is not one right way to heal. Our bodies are like highly sophisticated computers, each with its own nuances, hard drive, and programming. This is what Joshua Rosenthal, from the Institute for Integrative Nutrition, calls "bio individuality." He speaks of how one man's food can be another man's poison. As you travel your route to wellness, you will become more in tune with what you need, what serves you well, and what doesn't work so well. Listen carefully to the signals your body sends you, and watch what happens!

Below are some questions to ask yourself. If you keep a journal, jot these down, and as thoughts come to mind, capture them on paper. Take time to ponder them, maybe while sitting by a stream or on a walk in nature. Maybe meditation or yoga helps you to think more clearly. Whatever it is, make time for it, and give these questions and ideas the attention they deserve.

- How can you focus on living, rather than on your anxieties or limitations? What brings you joy? When do you feel most at ease? What makes you feel anxious? What can you leave behind, or release, that no longer serves you?

- What is in your control right now that you can change? What do you need help with? On whom can you lean for support? What resources do you have at your fingertips? As the founder of B-School, Marie Forleo always says, "everything is figureoutable!" Wellness guru, Kris Carr will say, "I learned it at Google University." Tap into what you need; there are resources at your fingertips!

- Who, or what, do you have faith in? How can you tap into that faith to support your healing? I encourage you to take the word "hope" out of your vocabulary and focus on knowing and believing; it will take you so much further on your journey! I once read a sign that not only made me chuckle, but also made me think about my own faith: "Write your plans in pencil and give God the eraser." More about this later!

- How can you take action? What are some simple steps you can take to unearth this root cause, and begin healing? How can you begin to make a difference, one step at a time?

- How can you shift your current thoughts or beliefs that are steeped in negativity, to those of gratitude, abundance, and happiness for the life you have?

There are many ways to approach unearthing the root cause to disease, some more conventional than others. I encourage you to keep an open mind and try new things. Below are just a few of the many avenues to consider and explore.

Life/Health Coach

Certified health coaches are trained in many facets of health and healing. They are wonderful listeners, and offer grounded suggestions specific to you. They will guide you in mapping out a plan for healing and living the life you deserve. There are many types of health and life coaches—some who specialize in chronic disease, like me, and others who target busy moms, or career and life transitions. Whatever it is you are struggling with, know that there is someone out there who has had a similar experience to yours, and can help you. Don't go it alone! A truly gifted coach will help you transition and heal!

Traditional Psychotherapy

I found this to be very helpful. When you find a really good practitioner, he or she listens intently, asks lots of thought-provoking questions, provides constructive feedback, and leaves you with more thoughts to ponder afterward. A therapist provides an objective set of eyes and ears that can offer another perspective, one that you may not have thought about on your own. You may need to see a few different therapists to find a good fit. The first guy I saw was a real creep! At first I thought I was the problem, then I realized that something just wasn't right; when I found someone really wonderful, I recognized the difference. I found someone I could trust, someone who truly believed in me and knew that I could thrive. Also, keep in mind that many psychotherapists have different specialties these days. I actually found someone who specializes in folks who suffer from chronic illness. When I first got started with her, I saw her weekly for several months–this was a big part of the "unearthing" process. Since then, as new challenges arise, I see her for what we fondly refer to as my "one-hundred-mile maintenance check." She has become a dear friend, and I look forward to our chats.

Less Traditional Psychotherapy

I have met other psychotherapists who take a more spiritual approach. Some even use what they call "spirit guides" to assist them in the process of supporting you on your journey. Although I come from a fairly conservative background, I kept an open mind, and found this to be quite a remarkable experience and a fascinating process.

Hypnotherapy

I used to think of hypnotherapy as the mind-altering experience that has often been portrayed in the movies–people being made to do things they would not normally do, and that are generally creepy. My opinion has since changed, after meeting with a friend who had obtained her certification as a hypnotherapist. She asked if I would be a "practice patient," and with some reluctance, I agreed. The process was such a delightful surprise! We started by chatting about one thing I wanted to accomplish, or a behavior I wanted to change. Together we wrote some simple objectives that would support my goals. She then had me get into a comfortable position, and she began talking in a soothing voice. Before I knew it, I was completely relaxed, yet quite aware of my surroundings and her voice. She took my goals and weaved them into a subtle message. She actually provided a recording of our time together that I could listen to whenever I was in a relaxed state. Doing this consistently not only provides a wonderful way to relieve stress, but is also a way to actually change unwanted behaviors and habits, and adopt new and healthy routines.

There are several other types of practitioners and practices that can assist in unearthing the root cause to disease, like past life regression and other forms of energy healing. Explore all the options readily available to you, and keep your mind open to trying something new!

Weed Out Your Obstacles

© heather rhodes

Chapter 3

"My path is clear and lined with beautiful blooms."

To give that newly planted seed a chance to grow, you must do some weeding to remove anything blocking your path in the direction you choose to go. Below are a few obstacles to consider throwing out with the garbage. Be objective and honest with yourself. Examine each one, and ask yourself if any of these, or other obstacles, are preventing you from leading the life you want to live. Get the shovel out, do some digging, and get rid of the weeds standing in your way.

Blame

I could have easily lived in a place of blame, blaming my father for what he did to me and allowing the abuse to ruin me for life, but I knew this was not the place I wished to dwell. I have seen others get stuck in this blame game, and stay stuck in the past. The best route to bypass the blame game is in forgiveness. Forgiveness is exceptionally healing–it is not a *feeling*, it is a *conscious choice*, one that will allow you to move forward and become the person you truly are. When you choose to let go of blame, it will release you from a sense of prison, and a heavy weight will come off your shoulders. I made this choice with my dad. It didn't excuse his behavior, yet it allowed me to move on, and begin loving him for his many qualities. We eventually became very close, and I finally had the dad I had always dreamed about. I'm not sure if my conscious choice to forgive him was the catalyst for his change in demeanor, or if he came to some awakening on his own, but whatever it was, I was extremely grateful for the outcome. If you are in a current situation of abuse (physical, emotional, or both), the first priority is to get help and be safe. Don't ever stay in a situation that allows someone to abuse you in any way. You can forgive from afar if need be. While I was at the healing institute I mentioned earlier, there was a young woman who was staying there for several weeks as a safe haven from an abusive boyfriend. It provided her with the protective shelter she needed at the time, and I believe she discovered her own true, lovely essence, and the road to a brighter future.

Fear

This destructive emotion encapsulated me for far too many years. I was burdened by my fear of my father, my fear of the dark, my fear of my dis-ease, and my fear of dying. I feared what others thought of me. I feared getting fired from my job. It was truly all-consuming. Don't get me wrong—in most cases, I had good reason to feel real fear. Yet I began to see that when we live in a place of fear, it is destructive to our health. Fear plays a role in your life—to alert you when something isn't right, is out of balance, or is seriously putting you at risk. Understanding what is driving the fear, and working to either eliminate the risk or put it into a proper perspective, are important to healing. Fear also arises when you feel out of control. The antidote to fear is to trust in yourself, in life, in a higher power. Through love, fear will dissolve and you will be safe.

To assist me in dissipating my fear, I did some work with my sister, who practices ThetaHealing. She asked me many questions, each one leading to the next. In the end, I could see that by trusting in a higher power, in the power within, and in love, there is no room for fear. Letting go of fear is like being unleashed. When fear tries to wiggle its way in, take a deep breath, believe in yourself, and trust in the process of life. You will find such a sense of peace when fear evaporates and is replaced with love. Whatever your fear is, don't allow it to own you; release it to the wind or to the clouds, or simply throw it out the window. Write your fear(s) on a piece of paper, crunch it up, and throw it in a fire or in the trash, where it belongs. For more on this, check out a blog from one of my greatest mentors, Louise Hay: www.healyourlife.com/let-go-of-your-fears.

Toxic Relationships

Do you have someone in your life that drains you? Someone who depletes you of your energy, or who keeps poking at your sense of self? Maybe someone who doesn't believe in your dreams, or even laughs at them? It may be a family member, a friend, a life partner, or spouse. Whoever it is, you may need to move away from that person, or learn to set serious boundaries in order to move on in your healing journey. You may be too close to this person, or too dependent, to see the toxicity of the relationship and how it is affecting you. Maybe your friends or family see it and are constantly badgering you about it. Sometimes we stay connected to someone out of fear—the fear of being able to support ourselves, the fear of standing on our own two feet. Maybe that person is an enabler who encourages an addiction or a path that simply isn't right for you. Are you in one or more relationships that no longer serve you and the life you want to lead?

If you answered yes, then it should be more than apparent who that person is in your life. If no one readily comes to mind, make a list of all of the people in your life (your friends, family, coworkers, your significant other), and next to each name list all of the positives and negatives that result from that relationship. If you see a pattern of more negative than positive, it may be time to rethink the role that person is playing in your life. You have a choice whether to stay in a relationship or not. You can also decide not to allow others to influence you in a negative way.

Depending on the severity of the toxicity, you may need to let someone go from your life all together, releasing that person with love. Making this choice can be very difficult and, soon after the release, you may think about that person on a daily basis. When this happens, it is important to have your list readily available to remind yourself why you made this choice, and what positive outcomes you expect to achieve without that person's influence. An important part of releasing someone with love is to send them good wishes through your thoughts. Although you may feel raw from the relationship, and have a strong desire to blame them, it will not serve you well to do so. I love the expression "what goes around comes around." I believe this with all my heart, and I embrace this little philosophy in life. When we hold a positive thought for another person, it will come back to us in some other avenue of life.

One of my favorite articles on this subject can be found on Kris Carr's blog, "How to Identify and Release Toxic Relationships," at www.kriscarr.com/blog-video/how-to-identify-and-release-toxic-relationships/.

A Draining Job

Are you praying for Friday to come sooner, and spending Sundays dreading Mondays? If this is you, then it's time to rethink what you do for a living. To me, the word *living* means doing what you love, and loving what you do! Getting paid for it makes it that much better. Like relationships, jobs can be toxic. It could be the boss, the work environment, the politics, harassment, or simply hating the work you do. If this is the case, then it's time to make a change, either within the company you are in, or by switching careers.

Some folks know they are working in a job that does not serve them well, and have a grand idea about exactly what they want to do, yet they are held back by the flow of money needed to pay the bills. Whatever the reason you decide to stay in a job that does not serve you well, it will eventually take a toll on your health and well-being. If you are not sure what you would like to do, there are wonderful career coaches out there who can help you unravel the thread to your dream career. In the meantime, try these exercises and see where they may lead you.

- Make a list of your strengths and then choose your top ten. Here is a sample list:
  1. Kind
  2. Generous
  3. Creative
  4. Energetic
  5. Organized
  6. Detail oriented
  7. Capable of leading
  8. Visionary
  9. Dedicated
  10. Honest

- Make a list of all the things you love, or love to do, things that make your heart sing! Here is a sample list:
  1. Animals & nature
  2. Cooking healthy food
  3. Teaching
  4. Helping/mentoring others
  5. Event planning and facilitation
  6. Gardening
  7. Hosting gatherings
  8. Theme planning
  9. Making jewelry
  10. Decorating
  11. Marketing
  12. Traveling
  13. Fashion
  14. Reading

- For the fun of it, once you have created a list of things you love to do, cut them out, place the items in a basket or bowl, and then draw out two at a time. Keep doing this until the container is empty. For each pair, write a paragraph about a career, new business, or type of work you could do that would involve both. This can be a blast, and might set you on the road to your next career! Here is an example:

  Traveling and Gardening—Develop a Garden Travel Tour. Research some of the most famous gardens in different parts of the world, and coordinate various types of tours for the public. Have four tours identified to repeat annually: Farm to Table Tour (Italy), Harvest to Oven Tour (France), Picnic in Parks Tour (New England), and Fun with Flowers Tour (Holland). Look back at your list of strengths to see how many of them would be utilized in this business concept. Have fun and enjoy!

Addictions

There are many forms of addiction. Whether it involves food or sugar, drugs or alcohol, addiction can be both physiological and emotional, and it needs to be professionally addressed. Don't go through this one alone. I have seen how destructive addictions can be on relationships, one's ability to work, and overall health and well-being. Addictions are a form of escaping from life's trials and tribulations, and they can stand in the way of achieving optimal health. They suppress our emotions and keep us from dealing with life. Reread the chapter on Unearth & Address Your Root Cause, which is critical to eliminating addictions (not just jumping from one form of addiction to another). You must address the underlying cause of the addiction, focus on the positive outcome you wish to achieve, and find support along the way to keep yourself on track. Check out Louise Hay's wonderful affirmations for addressing addictions: www.healyourlife.com/affirmations-for-addiction.

Excuses & Procrastination

Okay, so you know you want to make a change. You want to eat less, lose weight, start exercising, and so on, yet the proverbial excuses and procrastination set in. Then you're on the pity pot, feeling bad about what a failure you are for not doing what you said you were going to do! Yikes, what a vicious cycle we create for ourselves! I have to admit I am guilty, too. I get caught up in making excuses, but then I employ the famous Nike expression, "just do it." Suddenly I feel a huge relief, realizing that had I gone and just done it, I would have saved myself a whole lot of brain power and agony.

Here's the challenge: we often know what we need to do, but we constantly allow other tasks and obligations to get in the way of what we need or want to do. So you say to yourself, "I am going to improve my diet and start eating more vegetables." Then, when it comes time for lunch, you are in the middle of cleaning the house and on a roll, and don't want to stop and make the time to prepare something wonderfully healthy. Instead you reach for the preprepared junk food. Then the guilt sets in. Oh, what we do to ourselves!

I encourage you to make a list of everything you want to change or accomplish. Then go back and, without giving it too much thought, rank the items, with one being your highest priority. Depending on the complexity of your choices, commit to one to three key changes, and make a plan to prevent the excuse/procrastination syndrome. Let's go back to the lost lunch situation. If eating more veggies is on the list, then make a plan to prepare some veggie snacks and dishes in advance, essentially providing your own fast food. I do this twice a week; that way I don't have any excuses when hunger strikes, and I'm crazy busy doing something else. (More about this in chapter 4, Nourish Your ROOTS to Strengthen Your Core, *Food & Nutrition*.) A little planning and prioritizing will have you on track with your goals, help keep the excuses and procrastination from creeping in, and help you form new habits that will become positive changes for life.

Nourish Your Roots to Strengthen Your Core

© heather rhodes

Chapter 4

What did you do today...

1. To truly live?

2. To take care of you?

3. To live in gratitude?

4. To give to others?

5. To stretch your roots?

6. To show your love?

Positivity & Gratitude

© heather rhodes

Sub-Chapter 1

"I am grateful for the abundance in my life."

Many years ago a friend bought a book for me, *You Can Heal Your Life*, by Louise L. Hay. I'd notice the book on my shelf once in a while and think, "What a silly title for a book!" Little did I know that this book would send me on the road to healing my life! When I finally read the book, I read it again and again. I still refer to Hay's book when the inevitable curveball comes my way.

Don't get me wrong, the book itself did not heal me. The book inspired me to make a change in the way I looked at life. Because I was willing to do the work, be patient with myself, and take baby steps, a transformation began.

My turbulent past had set the stage for defensive behavior, distrust, pessimism, and incredibly pathetic self-esteem. Negative thoughts and self-talk kept me stuck in a downward spiral for years. With Hay's help, I began to change the negative thoughts to positive ones. It wasn't easy, but the positive thoughts worked like water that finds its way through the nooks and crannies of rocks and debris in a stream. My positive thoughts became more and more fluid, and found their way through the muck of negativity. The positive thoughts began to change my very definition of myself.

I stopped looking at myself as a victim, and began to unwrap the most precious gift of all: me. Despite all my emotional baggage and physical imperfections (scarred knees, short legs, wimpy hair), I was beginning to see and appreciate the real me. I discovered that I am made of love, passion, kindness, creativity—and lots of energy.

I'm still a work in progress. When I start being my own worst critic, I put the brakes on and remind myself how wonderful I really am. Okay, so to some of you this may sound like ego talking, yet I promise it comes from a place of love—a genuine love for myself, a love for life, a love for nature, and for you–every one of you! Healing begins with love. Love begins with loving yourself. Loving yourself begins with giving yourself positive messages—because your thoughts define your life.

As I was discovering the power of positive thoughts, I didn't know that I was actually changing the "attitude" of my genes. Say what? Yup, you heard me right.

It's called epigenetics. *Epi-* means surface, and *genetics* refers to your genes, your DNA, what you're born with. Scientists have discovered that many things can influence the way the surface of our genes express themselves. If you are genetically predisposed to a problem like heart disease, diabetes, or cancer, but you make many positive lifestyle changes, you can prevent or heal from these life-threatening illnesses. Those same genes will respond in a negative way if you are abusive to your body, and fail to take steps to make positive changes. For more on this, check out *Biology of Belief,* by Bruce Lipton.

Dr. Bernie Siegel's book, *Love, Medicine & Miracles*, is another wonderful resource about how what we think can make us sick—or heal us. In chapter 3, "Disease and the Mind," Siegel describes the mind–body connection, and the lack of recognition of this connection by Western medicine through the years. He describes how modern medicine has become so focused on healing through drugs that it has lost sight of people's inner strength and ability to heal themselves. Dr. Siegel goes on to describe the physiological processes through which our bodies listen to and respond to our thoughts, both conscious and unconscious. These thoughts affect the delicate balance of our sophisticated biological systems, and can disrupt hormones, the immune system, and the functioning of other organs. When our systems are out of balance, disease has an opportunity to take hold and make us sick! We have much influence on whether or not we allow this to happen. As my grandmother used to say, "Mind over matter!"

If your past leads you to negative self-talk, it's time to make a change. Start by making a list of all of your positive qualities down the left side of a piece of paper. If you're feeling down on yourself, go ahead and write what you believe to be the negative aspects of your character as well. For just a bit, give your negative judgments your full attention. Then transform these negatives into positives (for example, messy to organized, pathetic to lovable, sick to healthy).

Using these positive qualities, write a sentence in the form of an affirmation and say it often, at least daily. Examples: "I am lovable, worthy, perfect, whole, and complete. I am creative, energetic, and healthy. I am organized, and maintain a warm and inviting living space." You may find that the positives start bubbling up freely, and your list becomes longer and longer; keep it going!

This exercise is a great start, but for positive thoughts to take hold, you need repetition through daily practices. As positive thoughts become habits, they trickle through the negativity and dissolve it. I'm not suggesting this is automatic, but with time and patience, positive thoughts take root and change the trajectory of your life.

Choose from the following daily practices to keep your positive thoughts flowing:

- When you first open your eyes in the morning, say a few words of gratitude, something like this: "Thank you for a good night's sleep. I am grateful for my warm, comfy bed, and I am looking forward to a terrific day." Take a minute for a long stretch and a deep breath, and allow your senses to awaken to the new day, knowing that you are blessed to have this one perfect day ahead of you.

- As you reach the final stages of your morning routine, read or write a daily affirmation. Allow that affirmation's message to sink in, and plan how you may apply it throughout your day.

- When you take that final peek in the mirror, know you are ready to take on the world. Look into your eyes and say, "I love you; you are perfect just as you are." The first time I did this, it was hard and I felt quite silly. In fact, making eye contact with myself and saying that felt downright uncomfortable. Doesn't that speak volumes to my perceived self-worth? In time it became easier and, more often than not, I can now do this with sincerity. One thing that helped me was to imagine that little girl who was so abused—I looked at her with my adult eyes, and a genuine feeling of compassion and love emanated from within. Stick with saying those positive thoughts to yourself, and you will be amazed at what it will do for your self-esteem!

- Look for opportunities throughout your day to show random acts of kindness to others. Allow another car to pull out in front of you on a busy road; tell a coworker how great she looks in that color; offer to get someone a cup of coffee when you see she is having a busy day; ask, "How can I help?" Sometimes, just lend an ear and listen. On my ride to work I listen to a particular radio station, and the morning show has a great program where listeners call in with their "Feel-Good Story of the Day." Some of the stories are truly amazing, and leave me in awe of the kindness that is shown out there. Other stories are simple, yet every small act of kindness counts, and leaves a mark on humankind. I love this focus on the good that is happening all around us; each story causes an incredible ripple effect, encouraging others to make time for kindness. I truly believe that what you put out comes right back at you! What random act of kindness will you do this week?

- We all have stressful days from time to time. What I find helpful, when the stress level is high, is to visit a special place I have created in my mind. This is called creative visualization. My special place has become so clear and real to me that I can bring it to mind quickly and easily in times of stress. When I first began this process it was hard, but as I stayed focused, it became easier and easier. As I mentioned earlier, water is very soothing to me, so I chose a waterfall as the focal point of my creative visualization. I start out thinking about the look and feel and the sound of a waterfall. This waterfall flows into a small pool of water. I visualize a small ledge just inside the waterfall, where I lie to listen to the water flowing into the small pond below—this space feels safe, secure, and comforting. This pool of water has beautiful yellow, healing crystals floating on the surface. The water is surrounded by lush, green, tropical plants and flowers. In my mind, I arrive at this special place by walking down a winding dirt path surrounded by a beautiful forest. At the end of the path, and at the base of the healing pool of water, is soft green moss that feels pleasantly squishy between my toes. I can hear the sounds of birds, and am enamored of the beauty of the butterflies that come for a visit while drinking the nectar of the flowers. At the base of this little oasis is an outcropping of large boulders, which marks the entrance to a white sand beach, where the turquoise blue water is crashing onto the shore. I feel so at home in this Shangri-la that it is sometimes hard to come back to reality; yet when I do, I am completely relaxed, and my mind is recalibrated and ready for new positive adventures in life! Try creating your own special place and practice going there as often as you can, so when you are feeling out of sorts, you can visit this place easily.

- Keep a blank journal handy so you can express your feelings and list things for which you are grateful. Writing is such a wonderful way to sort through emotions, gain insight, and resolve problems. In the future, you can look back at what you've written. You will be amazed at how much you have grown, and what you have accomplished. Writing your dreams and desires is the first step in designing your future successes.

- When you climb into bed, exhausted from a long day, allow yourself to run through your day's events and make a mental note of everything that happened that day for which you are grateful. In addition, read a *love* letter to yourself, previously written by you, to you. It sets the stage for a great night's sleep. I share the one below with my clients, and encourage them to modify it and make it their own. It can really boost the transition from negative thinking to positive.

Love Letter

I live each day in the love of God, the light of the sun, the energy of the universe, and the great flow of the river. I am grateful for the abundance in my life of excellent health, wonderful friends, a career that I enjoy, and the financial prosperity that allows me to live comfortably and in harmony with my passions and desires.

I am perfect, whole, and complete just as I am, right now in this moment. I attract others into my life who are like-minded, and who love me just as I am. I make a conscious choice to forgive others for past injustices, and release old hurts and patterns within that no longer serve me.

It is my birthright to be well and healthy. I support this by my commitment to feed my body whole, clean food; to make time for great self-care; to make time daily to exercise; and to make time to do the things that I enjoy and that bring me great happiness. I look at the challenges that come into my life as opportunities to grow and learn. I am gentle with myself and, rather than criticize, I provide thoughts of encouragement. I look at each day as a blessing, and appreciate all that life has to offer.

Food & Nutrition

© heather rhodes

Sub-Chapter 2

"I love food that loves me."

simply love what I heard Dr. Mark Hyman say about food at one of his talks: "Our bodies are like complex computer systems, and our food is the software that programs the computer; it's the information that tells the body what to do." To me, this says it all! If we put junk in, we get junk out; and if we put good in, we get good out. I know this sounds simple, yet in a world that offers too many choices of prepared foods that are filled with dyes and preservatives, and coated with pesticides, it can be really tough to navigate what is and is not good for us. There is so much contradictory research that it can be very overwhelming and quite confusing. I believe this is a huge contributor to why so many Americans are grossly overweight, and struggle daily with chronic illnesses like type 2 diabetes, heart disease, and cancer. Much of this epidemic is directly related to the food ingested daily. Unhealthy foods are creating inflammation in the body, which then acts as a breeding ground for disease. This inflammation, over time, will flip on a switch in the body, triggering disease. To learn more about the science behind this, check out two of my favorite doctors; when it comes to scientific research, they really do their homework! Read the work of Dr. Mark Hyman, *The Blood Sugar Solution,* www.bloodsugarsolution.com, or Dr. David Katz, at www. davidkatzmd.com.

There is good news: Not only can we prevent many of these diseases, we can actually reverse them. Through good nutrition, those of us who were born with a genetic disorder or disease can optimize our health and live full, healthy lives. How can we do this? It's not with a pill, not with the latest fad diet, nor with extreme detoxes and cleanses. There is *no one-size-fits-all diet*! It takes educating yourself, committing to loving yourself enough to feed your body good foods, and developing new habits and routines with patience over time. *You can do it*!

I encourage you to work with an integrative health coach who can support you in customizing a plan specifically for you. As Hippocrates said, "Let food be thy medicine and medicine be thy food." If you have diabetes, then eating a low-glycemic diet rich in quality protein is critical to keeping your blood sugar stable. Remember my earlier comment about one man's food being another man's poison? Even a healthy food (like onions, for example) can cause an adverse re-action in some people. If you have many symptoms of inflammation in your system, like joint pain, severe allergies, high blood pressure, high blood sugar, and indigestion, then working systematically to eliminate and reintroduce certain foods can be very beneficial. Keeping a food journal can help when symptoms are severe. Be your own scientist through trial and error, and listen to your body. Your body will send you messages about what it needs, and what does not agree with it! As you work through this process and make positive changes, you will feel so much better, and your blood tests will show the proof in the pudding.

To get you started, I have created some dos and don'ts that I call "SEEDS" & "WEEDS." Post them on your fridge; keep a copy with you when you are on the road, or at work, as a quick reference guide. I encourage you to focus on the "SEEDS." Start with one or two a week, keep adding over time, and eventually the "WEEDS" will become extinct, crowded out by all the new blooms of vibrant health!

Living Foods

SEEDS: Eat lots and lots of sprouts, pea shoots, sunflower shoots, and microgreens. Don't be fooled by how tiny they are; they are jam-packed with nutrients. I include pea shoots and sunflower shoots in a daily juice I coined "Longevity Juice." The recipe is at the end of this section. (See *Recipe for Life* 1.) In addition, I put lots of sprouts in my lunchtime salad, or in a lettuce leaf roll-up, or in just about any recipe. Living foods are highest in phytonutrients, as they are still alive and growing when we eat them. These foods, when juiced, oxygenate the blood—it's like a shot of liquid gold to our bodies. *Juicing sprouts is one of the single best dos you can do for your health!* Learn more about the benefits of sprouts and living foods at the Hippocrates Health Institute: www.hippocratesinst.org/Products/sprouts-the-living-super-food.

WEEDS: Don't buy premade vegetable juices. If they have a shelf life, then they have something in them to preserve them, and that is not something you want to ingest. In addition, companies usually add sweeteners and other assorted "stuff" that is not good for you.

Vegetable Centric

SEEDS: Eat a rainbow of organic vegetables, preferablylocally grown. Locally grown are fresher, and typically do not have as many pesticides as those grown and transported from afar. Ask your local farmers about their growing standards and practices. The important thing is to increase the amount of veggies you consume on a daily basis! Frozen vegetables work too, in a pinch. Make three-fourths of each meal veggies! Eat veggies for a snack. Juice your lower-glycemic veggies. Eat a tablespoon of organic, cultured vegetables at each meal to aid in the digestion of your meal—these are fermented vegetables, which you can make yourself, or check out my favorites at Real Pickles:

www.realpickles.com/process.html.

WEEDS: Avoid what the Environmental Working Group (EWG) calls the "dirty dozen," which is their list of produce that has the highest pesticide residue. In addition, avoid genetically modified organisms or genetically engineered foods. Check out EWG's site for a list of conventional produce to avoid:

www.ewg.org/foodnews/summary.php.

Raw Versus Cooked Vegetables

SEEDS: Although most veggies are best eaten raw to maintain their nutrients, some—like sweet potatoes—are actually more nutritious when cooked. If you live in a cold climate, you need cooked vegetables as well to help keep you warm. Still, do your best to increase your raw veggie consumption, since they are the most nutritious. Prewash and chop raw veggies for a grab-and-go snack. They're great for dipping in hummus or guacamole.

WEEDS: For folks with a sluggish thyroid, there is some evidence that cruciferous vegetables, when eaten raw, may contribute to this condition. For a list of these veggies, check out this *Wikipedia* article: en.wikipedia. org/wiki/Cruciferous_vegetables.

Seasonal Vegetables

SEEDS: Focus on what is in season in your area for the freshest and healthiest veggies. This is easy to do when you shop at a local farmers' market, or are part of a CSA (community supported agriculture), which is usually a local farm where you buy into a share of the crop from that farm. In addition, there are many farm co-ops popping up where you can order online and have fresh, local produce delivered to your door. I do this weekly, and I am fortunate to have an arrangement with a farm that grows living foods! Otherwise, check out the website Field to Plate to find what's in season in your state: www.fieldtoplate.com/guide.php.

You can also freeze some of your favorite fruits and veggies to give yourself access to year-round local produce. When something is in abundance, like blueberries, pick extra and freeze them for a midwinter treat.

For seasonal veggie recipes, check out Terry Walters's cookbooks: *Clean Food, Clean Start,* and *Eat Clean Live Well at* www.terrywalters.net.

WEEDS: In today's market, we have available to us assorted fruits and veggies all year round. Having said that, most of the out-of-season fruits and vegetables come from afar, if you are living in a northern climate. They may be coming from outside the United States as well. The further they travel to your store shelf, the less nutritious they become. There is additional concern with some of the standard farming practices in certain countries.

Fruit

SEEDS: For ideal digestion, fruit is best consumed in the morning on an empty stomach, without other foods. Fruit should not be more than 15 percent of your diet, since it contains a lot of sugar. Go for lower-glycemic fruits like berries! Eat fruits either whole or in smoothies from time to time.

WEEDS: Don't juice fruit, because when you remove the fiber it will quickly raise blood sugar! If you have diabetes, cancer, or candida, it is best to avoid high-sugar fruits and, on special occasions, enjoy lower-glycemic varieties.

Sweeteners

SEEDS: Eat more whole, naturally sweet foods that will leave you feeling fuller, and provide all the wonderful nutrients your body wants and needs to be well. Fruit contains vitamins, minerals, and antioxidants that support the process of metabolizing the fructose. Berries rank highest on the health list; they are the lowest fruit on the glycemic index.

Experiment with other natural sweeteners that offer more nutrients. Use the following sparingly: raw honey, pure maple syrup, brown rice syrup, dates, coconut sugar, blackstrap molasses, and agave. All of these sweeteners can raise blood sugar and should be eaten in moderation (and minimally by diabetics). Other acceptable substitutes are stevia, erythritol, and Lakanto, which do not raise blood sugar.

WEEDS: Most Americans consume about thirty teaspoons of sugar everyday—that's about one hundred pounds a year! Yikes! Why do we consume so much of it? Well, it tastes good; consuming small amounts makes us want more; and when we quit cold turkey, we get headaches, cravings, mood swings, etc. Sound addictive? Sounds like it to me!

What is this granulated white stuff? It is a highly refined substance that is processed through charcoal filters. Rumor has it that it gets bleached! In the end, it has no vitamins, minerals, enzymes, or amino acids.

The end result of ingesting sugar is that it enters the bloodstream rapidly, causing spikes in your blood sugar. This causes the pancreas to work overtime producing insulin, which can lead to high triglycerides and type 2 diabetes. It also wreaks havoc on your immune system, and depletes your body of essential vitamins and minerals. Following the sugar high comes the sugar low, leaving you weary and exhausted.

Eliminate these pathetic, empty-calorie, disease-causing substances from your daily routine. *Read labels* and avoid the following: sugar, high-fructose corn syrup, brown sugar, confectioner's sugar, dextrose, and sucrose. Avoid artificial sweeteners altogether; many have well-recognized neurotoxins, and can cause a host of other issues.

For more info on this mission-critical health topic, check out this article at Wellness Today:

www.wellnesstoday.com/nutrition/do-you-have-the-sugar-blues.

Grains

SEEDS: For a happy gut, certain grains are a wonderful part of a daily diet. I choose grains that are higher in protein and lower on the glycemic index than some of the others. My top four are quinoa, millet, buckwheat, and amaranth. All of these grains are gluten free. Unless you purchase a sprouted grain, it is best to soak the grain for four to eight hours and then rinse well. I start my soak in the morning before work, then rinse and cook at dinner time. *Note: Buckwheat is not technically a grain; it is in the rhubarb family.*

Try substituting one of these grains in your usual recipes. Millet and amaranth are "mush-like" when cooked, and can be pureed into porridge. Both of these grains are mild, and will take on whatever seasonings you choose to use. I use sprouted quinoa in place of rice in most of my dishes. In addition, I use it to thicken soups or vegan chili. It is great in cold dishes as well, or as porridge. Buckwheat has a very strong flavor and may take some getting used to. My favorite is cream of buckwheat with a little ghee, cinnamon, and almond milk.

In place of a grain, I will often pulse a head of cauliflower in my food processor until it is the consistency of rice. I then steam it and season it as I would a rice dish. I also steam chunks of cauliflower, and then mash them like potatoes. Yum!

Most of my baked goods are made with finely ground organic nuts, like almonds and walnuts. Sometimes I use coconut flour as well. These flours are super high in protein, and will not raise blood sugar. Check out the Wellness Bakery www.wellnessbakeries.com for their mixes, or experiment with your favorite recipe, replacing regular flour with a nut flour. It may take a few tries to achieve the right consistency for baking. I find that using shredded zucchini or carrots in nut flour recipes, and adding an extra egg, helps keep the end product super moist. Experiment and have fun!

WEEDS: Many grains are high in carbohydrates and starch, and will raise blood sugar; they should be eaten in moderation. If you have any inflammatory condition, it is best to avoid grains with gluten (like wheat, rye, and barley). There are many others, so be sure to read labels and investigate online.

Here is a link to an article at the Whole Grain Council's website that may be helpful:

wholegrainscouncil.org/whole-grains-101/gluten-free-whole-grains.

Cooking Food

SEEDS: Lightly steaming or sautéing food is best. To maintain the best nutrient value, be sure not to overcook veggies. Other options are baking and lightly grilling, using caution to prevent browning and burning. Adding good quality fats and oils is best done after cooking. There is more about oils below. It's best to use glass pans for baking, and ceramic pans for sautéing.

WEEDS: Stay away from fried foods and overly cooked foods. Never heat foods in plastic, which releases toxic gasses. Avoid the microwave altogether. For more information on the hazards of microwave ovens, check out this link to an article at Mercola.com:

articles.mercola.com/sites/articles/archive/2010/05/18/microwave-hazards.aspx.

Also, stay away from nonstick Teflon pans. They, too, release toxic chemicals under heat. Avoid foods in cans and plastic bottles, unless BPA free. BPA is a chemical (bisphenol A) added to plastic containers and cans. Find more information at the Mayo Clinic's website:

www.mayoclinic.org/healthy-living/nutrition-and-healthy-eating/ expert-answers/bpa/faq-20058331.

Oils

SEEDS: High-quality organic oils such as olive, coconut, hemp, flax, unrefined sesame, and ghee (clarified butter) are an important part of a healthy diet. Most oils are best when not heated. Add oils after cooking for best flavor and nutrient value. Olive oil can be used over very low heat, but it is best not heated, as it can oxidize and lose its nutritional value. The best choices for oils under fire and heat are coconut and ghee. Never heat hemp, flax, or sesame oil. For occasional baking I will use coconut oil, ghee, or grapeseed oil. Hemp and flax oils need to be kept in the fridge. Check out this great resource on fats and oils at Mercola.com: products.mercola.com/coconut-oil/.

WEEDS: Don't eat anything with partially hydrogenated oils! They are to your heart what sand and gravel are to a working clock. Stay away from trans fats in general. Avoid overheating oils.

Nuts & Seeds

SEEDS: Nuts and seeds are such a wonderful part of a healthy diet, and great "on-the-go" snacks! Soak nuts in jars or bowls overnight, preferably each type of nut or seed in its own container. Rinse well. Either use in sauces or make nut milk immediately after soaking, or dehydrate them for 24 to 36 hours at a temperature of 110 degrees. Store in fridge for best shelf life. Nuts and seeds that do not need to be soaked are macadamia, pine nuts, chia, flax, and hemp. Some health-conscious stores carry sprouted, organic nuts and seeds—these are a great option when you don't have the time for soaking and dehydrating, although they can be expensive. For more information, check this out at the Food Matters website: foodmatters.tv/articles-1/the-benefits-of-soaking-nuts-and-seeds.

My favorite source for organic almond meal is at the website Nuts.com, www.nuts.com.

See *Recipe for Life* 2 for my "Grain-Free Crackers/Crust" recipe.

WEEDS: Not all nuts and seeds are created equal! Buyer, beware. Your typical supermarket nuts and seeds are not organic, and have not been soaked and rinsed, which means they still have natural yet toxic enzyme inhibitors. Most nuts are heavily sprayed with pesticides, too—especially almonds. Never use almond meal unless it is organic.

Water

SEEDS: Drink plenty of water throughout the day, more in the morning and less as evening approaches. A good rule of thumb is to drink half your body weight in ounces. So if you weigh 120 pounds, then you would drink an average of 60 ounces of water a day. Drink the highest quality of filtered water that you can. There are many filter options out there, so do your homework. If you are not a water fan, try "marinating" your water with lemon, cucumber and ginger, or mint and cucumber. Try different combinations to see what you like best and drink away! If you are on the road, choose a high-quality brand of bottled water such as Smartwater.

WEEDS: Don't drink unfiltered city water, or water that has a high chlorine or fluoride content. Also, beware of well water; it can test fine one day, and then become populated with assorted bacteria the next. In addition, well water is susceptible to runoff from pesticides sprayed for lawn care and weed control.

Other Beverages

SEEDS: Herbal teas, hot or cold, can be a great way to stay hydrated throughout the day, yet are not to replace your targeted water goals. If you like them on the sweet side, stir with a licorice root stick or add a few drops of a high-quality liquid stevia. Here is the link to the Hippocrates Health Institute, where I buy stevia: hippocratesinst.org/, go to the tab "store". Organic green teas, oolongs, and other fine organic teas have many health benefits, and one cup a day is a wonderful addition to your daily health regimen—as long as you can tolerate caffeine.

WEEDS: A glass of red wine has been noted for its health benefits, yet more than one glass can have the opposite effect. Not only is alcohol acidic, it is also high in sugar; therefore, it will contribute to that annoying, disease-causing inflammation. Worse than alcohol are sugary drinks, like soda and store-bought juice blends with added sugars. Even diet sodas are contributing to the epidemic of obesity in our country. There is some concern that the artificial sweeteners being used in these drinks may cause certain types of cancers.

Packaged Foods

SEEDS: Look for packaged foods with five or fewer ingredients. I look for one-ingredient foods, like organic cacao powder, which I use to make my own dark chocolate.

WEEDS: Don't eat preprepared or fast foods with preservatives, dyes, chemicals, etc. Here's some good advice: if you cannot pronounce an ingredient, or you do not know what it is, then don't eat it! If it is made in a lab, then most likely it is something we should not ingest. The longer the shelf life on a product, the more it will shorten *your* shelf life! Hmm, food for thought!

Animal Foods

SEEDS: High-quality, lean animal protein will help keep blood sugar in check. Only consume animal foods that are grass fed and antibiotic free. The portion size should be no larger than the palm of your hand. Look for lean cuts of meat. If you eat eggs, check out local farms and get fresh eggs from free-range chickens.

WEEDS: Stay away from processed meat, such as lunch meats, sausage, and ground meats with additives. Avoid eating mass-produced meats from farms where there are inhumane practices, where antibiotics are used, and where animals are fed genetically modified foods.

Food Combining & Food Synergy

SEEDS: There is so much cool research going on regarding the science of food synergy. When we eat broccoli with brussels sprouts, for instance, the result is an amazing enzyme that removes toxins from our body. Eaten together, rice and beans make a complete protein. There is so much more

to come on this topic… maybe in my next book! In the meantime, check this out at WebMD:
www.webmd.com/food-recipes/features/top-10-food-synergy-super-foods.

WEEDS: The science behind food combining fascinates me. Again, there is much research to come, yet I believe that anyone who suffers from an underlying condition caused by inflammation may want to consider playing with how they combine food. If you don't eat a protein with your grain, this will speed up the rate at which you digest your meal, causing less gas and bloating. Eating grain, or rich, starchy foods, separate from foods high in protein (like animal foods, nuts, and seeds) allows for optimal digestion and potentially greater weight loss. Check out the article at this great site, Body Ecology:
bodyecology.com/articles/food_combining_optimal_health_and_weight.php#.U_U442P5d5I.

Supplements

SEEDS: Supplements can be a wonderful way to support your overall health. There are some great products out there, sold by companies such as Vital Nutrients and the Hippocrates Health Institute. Look for products that are clean, not made with fillers or toxic chemicals. Get your blood work done and take only those supplements that you truly need to support your optimal health. I recommend working with a naturopathic doctor to review your personal requirements. A diet rich in nutrients, and an active lifestyle, are more of a magic elixir than anything you can find in a capsule.

WEEDS: There are many options for supplements out there and it is easy to be influenced by the extremely attractive media hype about one or another, promising to cure this or that! Unfortunately, too many of these products are not held to quality standards; their touted results are misleading, and the products may contain fillers and other chemicals that could contribute to further illness. When I was in the NIH's Undiagnosed Diseases Program, a young woman there was seriously ill due to toxicity from an overload of supplements. So, beware of falling under the spell of a "magic elixir" that promises to heal this, that, and the other thing! Know your source, do your homework, and listen to your body.

In summary, there is a great deal of nutritional information about food and how it interacts and affects our bodies, but the true test is in how it makes *you* feel. Really listen to what your body is telling you. If it is tired, sluggish, fatigued, depressed, or inflamed, then it is time to feed it what it needs to feel vibrant, well, and healthy! More to come on this, in another book.... For now, enjoy the following sample recipes.

Recipe for Life - 1

Longevity Juice

(I use an Omega 8006 juicer for high quality juice and ease of cleaning.)

Juice & strain the following organic vegetables & herbs:
- 1.5 C pea shoots
- 1.5 C sunflower shoots
- 1/2 C cilantro or parsley
- 1 C greens of choice
- 1 large cucumber
- 4 large stalks celery
- Other leafy greens can be added, but switch them up for various nutritional values
- 2" chunk gingerroot (optional)
- 1/2 lemon, with skin
- 1/2 green apple, seeds removed, or liquid stevia (optional for sweetness)

Drink (within 15-30 minutes of juicing) on an empty stomach. Swish or chew your juice for optimal digestion! This is a great way to start the day, but it is not meant as a meal replacement.

Recipe for Life - 2

Grain-Free Crackers/Crust

- 1 T ground chia seeds
- 1/4 C water
- 1 T grapeseed or olive oil
- 1/4 t baking soda (nonaluminum)
- 1/4 t sea salt
- 1/2 C ground flax meal
- 1 C ground almonds
- Bragg Organic Sprinkle Seasoning (24 herbs)

Whisk the chia seed with the water until it is "egg-like." Add oil, baking soda, and sea salt, and whisk until well blended. With a wooden spoon, stir in the flax meal and then the ground almonds. Mix until dough forms.

Place dough between two pieces of parchment paper and roll flat. Slide the dough onto a large cookie sheet. Sprinkle with the herb seasoning. Bake at 350° for 15-20 minutes.

This can be used as a pizza crust, or broken into small pieces for dipping or spreads.

Self Care & Your Environment

© heather rhodes

Sub-Chapter 3

"I believe in the magic of me."

So now that you are thinking good thoughts and taking care of yourself on the inside, let's visit the outside of you, including the world around you and how it affects your health. Let's start with your skin, the *largest* organ of your body! Your beautiful skin is kind of like a great big sponge, soaking up everything it comes in contact with, including the air we breathe, beauty products, moisturizers, cleaning products, chemicals used to manufacture clothing, and sunscreen. If you apply or are exposed to products with toxic chemicals, those toxins are being absorbed through your skin, and could very well be making you sick from the outside in!

I am as nutty about buying organic products for my skin as I am about the food I eat. An excellent resource for knowing what's in a product and if it is considered safe is the Environmental Working Group's Skin Deep database: www.ewg.org/skindeep/. There is even an app you can download to your mobile phone, so if you are out shopping and considering a product, you can check out how it ranks for being clean and safe to use. If funds are tight, I suggest that when you finish a product you are currently using, replace it with something healthier. If you can afford to do so, get a clean start and do a makeover on all your products.

My favorite self-care tip, which is so healthy, does your skin wonders, and is ridiculously affordable, is coconut oil. Yup, the stuff you cook with! I buy only organic, and always get whichever one is on sale. This is something you can purchase in the healthy section of most grocery stores. It costs about ten dollars a jar, and can replace all your expensive moisturizers and eye creams. The best way to use this yummy product is to scoop out a chunk about the size of a walnut, and apply it immediately after your shower or bath, while still wet. Using your fingertip, gently rub some under your eyes, then coat the rest of your body, working from the tips of your appendages to your heart center. This not only keeps your skin moist, it helps stimulate your lymphatic system to do its job. Once you are all oiled up, pat yourself dry with a towel. In addition to keeping your skin soft, radiant, and healthy, it is also a natural sunscreen (not for sunbathing, however). I love the way coconut oil makes my skin feel and smell. Even during one of the toughest winters recently, my skin never felt dry and itchy! In addition, I use it in my hair, allowing it to sit while I take a bath, then I shampoo it out. My hair is so shiny after a treatment with coconut oil! I guess you could say I'm cuckoo for coconut oil!

Here's a big word of caution on the use of antiperspirants that are made with aluminum. There has been an abundance of research on varying health issues that can arise from using this one product, including breast cancer, Alzheimer's, and kidney disease. There are studies that point the finger at this product we use every day, and there are studies that say it is hogwash. It is hard to know what is right in these cases, but in my opinion, why mess with it? If it is a chemical that is linked in any way to a health risk, don't risk it! I have found a few natural deodorants that do a great job of preventing the bacteria that make us smell, but do not prevent us from sweating, which is fine with me, since it is good to sweat—it releases toxins from the body.

Be a product detective and look at the cleaning supplies you use. I once realized that the cleaning product I was using on my wood floors was causing my dog to have seizures. I now use a natural product, and guess what, no more seizures! It is amazing how toxic these chemicals can be. Some are considered carcinogens. Consider what you use to wash dishes, launder your clothing, wash windows, and so on. Use the EWG site and learn about the alternatives. If one product doesn't do the job, then try another, until you find one that is both safe and effective. You can also search Google for homemade solutions, like mixes with white vinegar, which is a great cleaner. The less ingredients the better, and using clean and healthy ingredients keeps you clean and healthy!

An often overlooked hazard to our skin is the clothing we wear. I never would have imagined that clothing could be toxic to my health until I read the book *Killer Clothes*, by Brian and Anna Clement, codirectors of the Hippocrates Health Institute. So much of the clothing available to us in the United States is being imported from China, and before leaving China the fabrics are sprayed with formaldehyde. Even after several washes, the toxic chemical continues to leach from the fabric into our porous skin. I now also avoid synthetic materials made with plastics, chemicals, and harsh dyes. Being a fashionista, I love clothing, and have now challenged myself to find "clean clothes" that are not toxic, yet fashionable. I have found many sites online that make cool organic clothing with natural materials like cotton, silk, hemp, and wool. Here are a few of my favorites:

1. Spiritex, www.spiritex.net/;
2. Synergy Organic Clothing, www.synergyclothing.com/;
3. Bgreen apparel, *www.**bgreenapparel**.com/* ;
4. Blue Canoe, www.bluecanoe.com/.

The most important articles of clothing for women are the undergarments we wear. Most wear bras made with synthetic materials that contain harsh chemicals and plastics, and include metal underwire for support. With the epidemic of breast cancer, I highly advise rethinking your bra! Skip the underwire and go with organic cotton. You won't believe how comfortable they are, and yes, they even provide support. These organic bras are getting better and better. Check out the following sites for clean bras:

1. Blue Canoe, www.bluecanoe.com/collections/organic-womens-lingerie,
2. Bgreen apparel, *www.**bgreenapparel**.com/,*
3. FaeriesDance.com, www.faeriesdance.com/bras-camisoles-c-25_15_14. html?page=all&sort=5a.

Sunscreen has become controversial of late. We hear all the time: don't go out in the sun without slathering yourself in sunscreen. Yet these sunscreens are filled with toxic chemicals, and may be causing certain types of cancers. At the same time, the sun is strong, and getting burned is not healthy for your skin and overall health.

The sun is your friend when you take certain precautions. If you are sensitive to the sun, wear a sunscreen that is approved by EWG, or wear lightweight, natural fiber clothing. The best sun exposure is in the early morning, or early evening as the sun is setting. We need some sun each day to gain a daily dose of vitamin D_3, which is critical to absorbing calcium for strong bones. Without D_3, calcium can cause our bones to be more brittle. Get your vitamin D levels tested, and if you live in northern climates, you will likely need to supplement this important vitamin. The best protection from the sun lies in foods you eat. A clean, healthy diet can protect you from all kinds of cancers. When you feed your body foods rich in antioxidants, minerals, and vitamins, while avoiding harmful fats, sugars, dyes, food additives, and chemicals, you set the stage for protection from disease from the inside out.

Another area of self-care that many of us take for granted is disconnecting from electronics and media. I call it "Bad Vibes and Bad News Syndrome." There are the physiological effects from all the electronics in our world, and psychological effects from all of the bad news, violence, and emotionally draining tales being told. When I see folks with cell phones plastered to their heads, it makes my stomach sick, knowing they are pumping all that electrical energy into their brains. Disconnecting from your cyberworld and reconnecting with nature will support balance in your body, both emotionally and physically. When I hear that someone is suffering with depression or anxiety, this is one of the first things I recommend. Get outside, wiggle your toes in the grass or dip them in the water, sit under the shade of a big tree and read a good book, while drinking a cup of herbal tea. Listen to the birds and the insects, and enjoy a moment without the business of your day-to-day life!

I know how busy you can be with work, family obligations, and community commitments. But if you run yourself ragged, you cannot give your best to anyone else. Make sure you make time for a leisurely bubble bath, a therapeutic massage, a long walk on the beach, and whatever else that brings you pleasure and joy. When you make these activities a priority, you are sending yourself a strong message that you are worthy, that you are important, and that you are truly loved. Now go find something that is just for you!

Put a Little Wiggle in Your Walk

© heather rhodes

Sub-Chapter 4

"I am happy, healthy, and whole."

Unlike a dedicated athlete or fitness guru, the average person gets little, if any, exercise. We spend much of our time parked in front of a computer, seated at a desk, or crashed on a couch watching TV or playing video games. When not doing these things, we are likely feeding our faces with junk food! This is a combination for disaster to our health and well-being.

If you are like me, exercise is usually your last priority; so we need to be clever to make time for it daily. Exercise is critical to your health. It keeps your digestive track running more smoothly; it also keeps your joints happy, your lymph system active, and your bones healthy. In addition, exercise does wonders for your state of mind, and helps with depression and anxiety. Physical activity is excellent for your overall health, when it is done right.

When I see folks running on any type of pavement, I cringe; this is one of the worst things you can do to your joints. Your body is not built for pounding on hard surfaces; it wears away at the cartilage and bones. If you enjoy running, stick to running on natural surfaces as our ancestors did long ago! I believe that by walking, you can accomplish the same results and save your joints. The important thing is to get moving!

Rather than going out and buying cute exercise outfits, or joining a gym that you may use once or twice, try keeping it simple and then gradually adding to your routine. Walking is wonderful, even if it's just for ten minutes a day. Take your dog for a walk; set an alarm to remind yourself to take stretch breaks at work; add a midday walk during your lunch break; park far from your destination to get in some extra steps; take the stairs rather than the elevator. In inclement weather, if you don't own a treadmill or elliptical machine (which, by the way, you can pick up cheaply online if you buy a used one), you can stop at an indoor mall and walk a few rounds before heading home.

Swimming is certainly one of the best forms of exercise. It is so forgiving to your joints and muscles, and yet such a powerful aerobic exercise and muscle builder. Here's a word of caution, though: if you are using a pool, inquire about what the facility uses to keep it clean. If they are using harsh chemicals, then I would stay out of that water. Some pools are filled with salt water, and are treated with ozone to keep them clean; this is wonderful water in which to swim. At the Hippocrates Health Institute they have many pools, one of which is a mineral pool, which is so healthful and relaxing!

Keep a few handheld weights around the house and use them while chatting on the phone, watching TV, or waiting for that pot of water to boil. I hired a personal trainer a few years back who gave me a simple list of items I could pick up at the store: weights, stretchy ropes, and a yoga ball. She taught me how to use them for stretching, toning, and building muscle. This trainer specialized in helping folks who are recovering from an injury or who have specific physical limitations. I learned so much from her! I hired her for three sessions at seventy-five dollars each, which was money so well spent. Now I have this valuable information for life, and can use it when it fits my busy schedule. Consider hiring your own trainer to be sure you learn the correct way to use these simple tools, and then make a plan to use them as part of your daily routine. This is a great step toward preventing osteoarthritis and other joint and bone issues.

Any chance I get to dance, I take it! I love music and I love to dance the night away. Sometimes I even just put on music at home, all by myself, and dance up a storm. Hey, no one is there to watch, and I can be as silly as I want. It makes me feel so good! Give it a try—put your favorite music on and dance, dance, dance! I also love being out in nature, and I frequently choose hiking and kayaking for my recreational exercise. Find what works for you, and get that wiggle going!

My last but not least important recommendation for exercise is to not go it alone. Set regular dates to walk with friends. Join a Meetup group that has a focus on a physical activity that you may enjoy: www.meetup.com/. Many of the Meetup groups are free, or have a minimal fee to join. It's a great way to meet new friends. If you have a life partner, choose something that you would enjoy doing together and make it a date night. Invite a friend to join a class with you such as yoga, tai chi, Pilates, or spinning. Many of these programs are offered at local churches or community organizations. Check your local paper, or look online for adult education classes near you.

The most important thing is to get moving! Don't be a weekend warrior, or go from zero to a hundred. Take small steps, try new things with care, and find a partner to keep you motivated. Commit to exercise because you are worth it; your energy will increase, and your health will continue to improve each day!

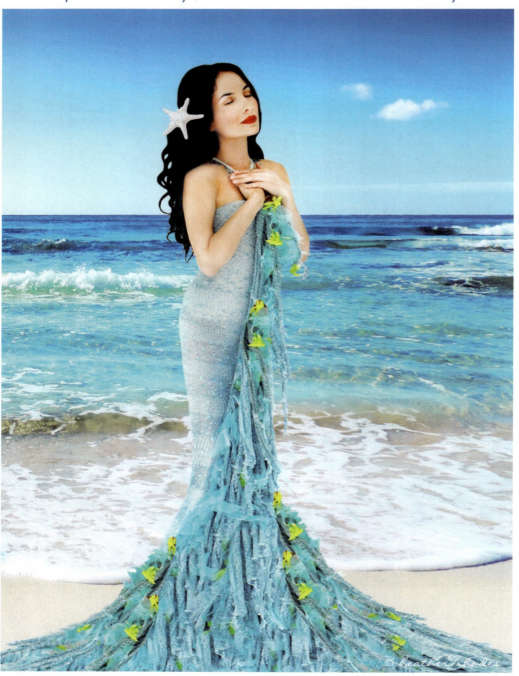

Spirituality, Love & Creativity

© heather shades

Sub-Chapter 5

"My dreams are woven with spirit, creativity, and passion."

believe that spirituality, love, and creativity are one. When we are deeply connected to our inner spirit and the great energy that surrounds us, we can live in a state of love; then creativity flows freely. I think spirituality is personal and unique to each person. What matters is that you embrace it in the form that feels right to you.

Most of my life I felt devoid of any spiritual connection; it wasn't until my health began to erode that I sought out a higher power, which I call God. I think of God not as a person, but as a never-ending energy that surrounds me in love. I draw on this regularly, and have developed a deep faith that provides great comfort. I have come to recognize God in many forms. I see God in the eyes of another, in random acts of kindness, in the flow of the river, in the blossom of a flower, in the invention of another. I believe that everything—both good and bad—happens for a reason. I believe we are given exactly the lessons we need in life when we need them. Sometimes we have to hit rock bottom to recognize the lesson being served up to us.

When fear starts creeping in, I call upon my inner strength and this universal energy to lift my spirits, and I say to myself, "This will pass and all is well." I start and end my day noting what I am thankful for, and I express my gratitude for the abundance in my life. I feel protected and safe. I believe that this universal energy I call God flows through me, and I am part of a greater whole. As I mentioned earlier, I believe that God is love and love is what fuels us to be well, to live well. When we live in a state of love, our actions will follow suit, spreading kindness and joy to others.

I also ask for what I need, for myself and for others. Sometimes I ask a question, and within a day or two, sometimes immediately, I have an answer before me. When someone I love is hurting, I hold them in my prayers to God, asking for a solution, for healing. I know that if the person is receptive, that universal energy will provide them with the answers they need. There are times when I don't know what I need and I am unsettled, so I ask God to take my hand and lead me to where I need to be, to show me the way. Again, the direction comes, yet not always in the form I expect; this is something I have come to appreciate over time.

We are all unique. There is only one you and only one me, yet we have this universal energy and love that flows through us, making us one. It is such a gift when we recognize the flow of this energy and, in turn, what makes us unique flows from us into whatever creative means we are blessed with. You may be a painter, a jewelry maker, a dancer, an interior decorator, an engineer, or a teacher. Whatever it is you do as a career or a hobby, when you open up to this flow of energy, the creativity will effervesce from deep within.

When I began my spiritual journey, I explored various organized religions and found a wonderful sense of community, yet I still felt something was missing. I then began devouring books on religion and spirituality; and, like a seed emerging from the ground, I began to see a glimpse of light. When I reached out to friends and family, they quickly became my mentors in this journey, and I grew even more toward the light. When I looked inside and invited this God, this energy, to reside within me, the most amazing bloom began to unfold. I encourage you to explore, seek, question, trust, and believe. Your bloom is within, just waiting to emerge!

© heather rhodes

Sub-Chapter 6

"I am surrounded with love and support."

Although I advocate that the power is within you to fully heal, that doesn't mean you need to go it alone. For your best success, surround yourself with support. I get my support from family, friends, assorted practitioners, God, and my beloved pooch. Having said that, beware of well-meaning friends and family who insist that you need more of this, or more of that. Or practitioners who insist you need to take a medication to heal, and that it is the only option.

The best support is from folks who wish to be partners in your healing journey, not dictators!

When I first took control of my health, I became very defensive when others tried to insist I do things a certain way, or that what I was doing was wrong. Now I am able to listen, sometimes learn new information that may help me, and respond from a position of kindness and confidence. I can even say, "Thank you for that information, I will take it into consideration," or "I'm so happy to hear that is working for you." I no longer go into why I do this or that a certain way, unless, of course, they ask for their own personal growth. I have learned to surround myself with those who want to be my partner in this, and I keep those who do not at a respectful distance, and have learned not to share certain information with them. I am now in control of my health (with lots of love and guidance from a higher source), and feel blessed to help others do the same!

If you are currently working with a practitioner who is being more dictator than partner, ask that person to be your partner in your healing, and to be open to alternatives and your thoughts about your illness and your preferred course of healing. If the practitioner does not get onboard, then interview—yes, interview—another practitioner who can be your partner in healing. Keep in mind that doctors are service providers. They are a valuable source and wealth of information, yet they do not know all of the answers, and they are human beings who come with their own set of opinions and life experiences that influence their style of treatment. Ask friends for recommendations, especially friends who have had their own healing journeys. I would also recommend seeking a functional or integrative medicine doctor—they are more open to bridging conventional and natural medicine. Here is a great resource for finding a doc near you, at the Functional Medicine Institute's website: www.functionalmedicine.org/practitioner_search.aspx?id=117. Or you can use Google to search for integrative medicine in your home town or state.

Before going to see a new doc, prepare for your visit. Type up all your symptoms, all the meds and supplements you have tried and are currently on, all the tests you have had and the results. Bring records with you. Whenever you have tests done, request a copy of the results and keep them in a designated file, in chronological order. In addition, search Google for your particular symptoms or diagnosed disease to learn about the latest research and course of treatment. (If you have an unusual or rare disease, check out the National Organization for Rare Disorders at www.rarediseases.org.) Print articles that are of interest, and then create a list of questions to ask your doc during your visit. Be your own detective—don't rely on the doc to do this work. More often than not, conventional practitioners, due to insurance constraints, can only spend a certain amount of time with you. If you see multiple docs, ask all of them to collaborate with one another, or at the very least to "cc" each other on test results and the like.

I now have an amazing team of docs on my team. Each has something different to offer, and yet all of them keep open minds and give me their full support. I like it when I ask questions and they are not afraid to say, "I have no clue," or "that's not something I have heard of." They are not afraid to be real with me, and they stay open-minded to the things I want to explore. Right now my team consists of my primary care doc, who has training as an osteopathic doctor; my pulmonologist, who is both a clinician and a research doc; and my naturopathic doctor, who is also a pharmacist.

In addition to my team of docs, I have many wonderful practitioners who I see, on occasion, for refueling, reenergizing, resetting, clearing, and basic care and comfort. They include an acupuncturist, a massage therapist, and someone who specializes in energy medicine. All of these treatments keep my energy moving, and help to clear any stuck or stagnant "toxic waste" in my system, which leaves me feeling like a million bucks! Having them in my wheelhouse of healing is critical to my overall wellness, and sends a clear message to me—"I am worth it!"

So who is in your court, who do you need to weed out and add in? Get clear on your goals, and who can support them. Don't be afraid to keep refining this list until you create your own dream team of supporters!

Bloom Your Route to Wellness

© heather rhodes

Chapter 5

"I stand tall and radiate success."

Whether you are just getting started on your healing journey, or you have been at it for a while without success, knowing where to begin can be overwhelming and frustrating. It takes great patience, discipline, and lots of love to heal. I encourage you to take baby steps, and give yourself credit for even the smallest successes. Success breeds more success, and makes you feel more eager to stay on track. For most of us, our conditions are the result of years of poor diet, bad habits, and a lousy day-to-day lifestyle. The longer you have been unhealthy, the longer it may take to heal, so patience is a critical tool to have in your toolbox. Having said that, our bodies are very forgiving and eager to heal, so as soon as you begin nourishing your *roots*, your body starts listening and the healing begins.

This book is filled with many tips, yet the one that is critical to healing is changing your thought patterns from negative to positive. Whenever you hear yourself saying, "I can't do that. That is beyond what I am capable of. It won't work for me because...," change this thinking to, "I can do that! I am capable of that and more! It will work for me because...." I also recommend changing the word "hope" to "know." Don't "hope" to get better; "know" you will get better. You get the idea! Negative thinking is a pattern that takes time to change, yet the results are beyond incredible. When we think in positive terms, everything seems doable, and we tackle tasks with enthusiasm and confidence.

Remember, you are human, and this is a very human experience in which you are engaged. There will be times when you slip into old patterns and habits, but don't beat yourself up; just get back on track, and remind yourself how far you have come! It is so easy to see the yucky stuff in life when it happens, and we lose sight of all the wonderful progress. This is when it is great to have a journal to reference, to see how far you have come, to look back and recognize your amazing accomplishments. Keep them going!

In addition to your journal, you may wish to create a vision board of what you want your life to look like. My vision board has pictures of the types of foods I want to eat, of places that I long to travel to, of activities like gardening and making jewelry, of the many powerful mentors in my life whom I idolize for one reason or another, and the type of home and environment in which I want to live, work, and play. Another visual tool that delivers awesome reminders is the sticky note message. You can make one for the fridge, with a reminder of the snacks you have readily available when hungry; one on the vanity mirror, with a message saying, "I love you as you are"; another on your car dashboard, saying, "Today will be a wonderful day." You can also leave these for family members. I used to write positive notes on my son's napkin in his lunch box; at lunch time I would get a warm feeling, knowing he was reading my little note to let him know how much he's loved.

As you set out on this healing journey, create your own road map to follow. Be prepared for detours, but having a route to follow will help you to stay on course. As you develop this road map, keep in mind the importance of unearthing and addressing the root cause, the imbalance in your body that created this condition; include a plan to weed out and address any obstacles standing in your way to healing; and fill your garden with many ways to nourish your roots for a vibrantly healthy bloom!

In wellness and in love,

Janet

With Gratitude

➤ *To Lindsey Smith and Joshua Rosenthal at the Institute for Integrative Nutrition, for their outstanding leadership and guidance in this book writing process. www.integrativenutrition.com*

➤ *To Bonnie Budzowski at Incredible Messages, for her encouragement and support in drawing the true message out from under years of experiences and emotion. www.incrediblemessages.com*

➤ *To Betty Devlin, my proofreader, who painstakingly read my book word for word, providing better flow and fixing all the boo-boos.*

➤ *To Heather Rhodes at Studio Petronella, for her brilliant and highly creative graphics and design.*
www.studiopetronella.com

38845661R00046

Made in the USA
Charleston, SC
17 February 2015